21 Ways to Break Through to Massive Success with Your Next Project

21 WAYS

to **break through** to
massive
success
with your
next project

MaryAnn D'Ambrosio, Ph.D.

High Point, North Carolina

21 Ways™ Series, Book 10

Published by Discover! Books™
an Imprint of Imagine! Books™
PO Box 16268, High Point, NC 27261
contact@artsimagine.com

Imagine! Books™ is an enterprise of Imagine! Studios™
Visit us online at www.artsimagine.com

Copyright © 2012 MaryAnn D'Ambrosio
Cover Design © 2012 Imagine! Studios™
Illustrations by Drawperfect, purchased at istockphoto.com

All rights reserved. No part of this publication may be reproduced
or transmitted in any form or by any means, including informational
storage and retrieval systems, without permission in writing from
the copyright holder, except for brief quotations in a review.

ISBN 13: 978-1-937944-15-5

First Discover! Books™ printing, April 2013

Dedication

This book is dedicated to you. It's an honor and delight to be of service to you and your business. My deepest desire in writing these 21 Ways is to see you thrive and prosper in all aspects of your business and life. I can picture it now: You, fully embodying your gifts and talents, taking action that's aligned with your vision and successfully sending your magnetic message that draws in ideal clients. You've stepped into your power!! By doing so, you become the person that energizes and inspires others to their greatness!

Acknowledgements

A giant thank you to the countless teachers and mentors who throughout my life have imparted knowledge, wisdom, and inspiration!

Bouquets of gratitude to my publisher, Kristen Eckstein of Discover! Books, and the many amazing entrepreneurs and visionaries who in their own unique way have contributed to the creation of this work: Jadwiga Pylak, Gina Carucci, Bob the Teacher Jenkins, Caterina Rando, Daphne Bousquet, Jacqueline Wales, Chris Makell, Soleira Green, Jennifer McLean, Felicia Slattery, Michelle Casto, and D'vorah Lansky.

Most significantly, I am eternally grateful for the love and support of my family and dear husband, Jack. While encouraging me to follow my mission, he's the one who rarely takes an intermission. Jack, I truly appreciate everything you do to make our life together beautiful. It's such a joy to be with you on this journey of self-discovery!

Introduction

It's so exciting to be part of the "21 Ways" series and introduce a new approach to creating massive success for your next project. Are you ready to advance or start a "new" project? Whether it's creating an information product, writing a book, developing a program, organizing a conference or hosting an online event—just to name a few—you'll find the Ways in this book innovative, energetic, and practical. The key to achieving phenomenal results with your next project is to begin applying the Ways that resonate with you today.

Sure it's important to have a vision and take action, and the support of a team to actualize that "dream" project is equally vital. But perhaps the most crucial aspect of your success is what happens when you're faced with unexpected challenges and insurmountable obstacles *during* your project. Do you become frustrated, overwhelmed, and allow your stress level to spike?

A secret to success that is often ignored is your state of emotional and mental well-being. What if you could consistently apply Ways to remain calm, centered, and clear even when you're faced with difficulties? In addition to improved productivity, greater performance, and staying on schedule, you would have access to priceless well-being. The most successful business professionals and entrepreneurs employ the value of energetics—an inner power source—to their projects. It's the passion, focus, confidence, inspiration, and "renewable" energy that allow them to carry out their projects with grace and ease.

Projects require a ton of directed energy and you'll want to make several of these Ways, such as the R&R Way—Reflection and Relaxation—an important part of your daily practice. Rest assured (no pun intended), you will see instant benefits.

My intention in writing this book is to provide you with inner and outer *"energizing"* Ways to create successful projects and prosperous results. Be sure to check out the "Resources in this Way" sections at the end of each Way to further spark your imagination and ignite your inspiration.

Here's to supercharging the success of your next project or event!

~MaryAnn

Create an Experience

Let's say your next big project is to create an in-person event like a summit to help business professionals "Thrive in the Midst of Change." How do you set your event apart from others? The more actively involved a participant is in multi-sensory learning, the more memorable *your* event is. And, frankly, the more successful and financially rewarding your business will be. Research shows that people are willing to pay more for an experience.

You've probably heard the expression: "To achieve specific results, be intentional." There's tremendous power in setting a specific intent for your event. Intent is more than a goal; it's a powerful, yet invisible, driving force that fuels the overall experience and results for you. Interestingly enough, you've also got the power to energetically set the environment for the audience, joint venture partners, and your potential clients.

Intent means knowing what you want to experience and directing your actions toward that outcome. By stating the intent, you gain the support of your subconscious mind to create the prosperous results that align with your heart's desire and overall goal. Using the "Thrive in the Midst of Change Summit" example from above, the intent for this event is to provide rich content that's transformational and inspirational, one that allows participants to take purposeful action to thrive.

The key element in creating a memorable event is *pre-designing the "desired" event experience and outcome.* Begin with the end in mind. It may sound like a tall order, yet you're already pre-designing life outcomes either by default or design. (Play with intent daily to consciously create everything in your life by design, including relationships, health, wealth, independence, and overall prosperity!)

To pre-design your event experience, place your awareness on the look and feel of the outcome. Now you're ready to tune into the "experience" and "why" success elements outlined below for your next project.

Success Element 1: What would you like to happen?

What type of event experience do you want to intentionally create for *you* and others?

- ✓ Your *audience*
- ✓ Your *speakers*
- ✓ Your *sponsors*
- ✓ Your *support team*
- ✓ Your *joint venture partners*

Remember, you're thinking in terms of the big picture that's in complete alignment (Way 8) with who you are and what your business brand represents.

Success Element 2: Identify your "why"

Why do you want to create this event? (Note: There needs to be a compelling why. If it's only for "the money" without a bigger purpose, there's a high probability your results will be less than stellar.)

Have you ever noticed that when you intend to do something, you're "on purpose" and there's a different energy that fuels the results? Put pen to paper and use the "experience" and "why" success elements you identified above to complete the following statement: *"My intent for the event is . . ."*

By declaring your power-filled intent, you've set into motion the energy to create the experience. Now it's up to you to take the action steps to make it happen.

Catch the Inspiration

It can be fleeting and elusive, yet when a connection is made with inspiration, it's like adding rocket fuel to roller skates. In addition to firing up momentum for your next project or event, watch yourself take off, too. Inspiration feeds your spirit and serves up more creativity, joy, and fun in both your personal and professional world.

So often our days are filled with busyness and serious thoughts about the "have-tos" on our to-do list. Let's take a break and play for a minute. Imagine owning a "joy" meter—a gadget that reads your level of happiness and enjoyment. Stop for a moment and take a reading. On a scale of 0 to 10 (with 10 being absolute bliss), what's your level of joy at this moment? Chances are you would welcome more joy in your life.

Most adults have forgotten what joy feels like. Young children live it. They smile, laugh, sing, dance, and really know how to shine. Their hearts are open, filled with happiness, peace, and a sense of excitement. Joy glows from within and expands in all directions. What would bring you joy today—getting out to play?

With so much on our overfilled plates, oftentimes we're "too full" to play. And play is exactly what we need. Consider it your lucky day. Playfulness has knocked on your door, encouraging you to come out and have some fun. If you're taking yourself, your work, or your life too seriously, it's time to lighten up. Put on your play shoes and enjoy the freedom that is yours for the taking! Step into lightheartedness, good humor, and a high-spirited state of being. That's where brilliant ideas and breakthroughs are located.

Catch the inspiration

Get out in nature, take a walk by the water, doodle, sing a little ditty, laugh, giggle, do a silly dance, and you'll quickly feel more lighthearted. Major breakthroughs tend to happen when you let go and have fun. Playfulness is contagious! In other words, as your team, clients, prospects, and colleagues notice that you're in a lighthearted space, the other "big kids" will want to join in. What if "many giggles each day keep you and your business healthy." We know it's true: "Laughter is the best medicine." Go ahead, catch the inspiration and connect with your playful side—it does a body, mind, and spirit good!

Organize Your Brilliance

Great ideas tend to quickly pop in and out of the mind. When you have a lot going on, press the *pause button*—take time to map out the plan! The more organized and focused you are on what's happening in the present, the less stress and more energy you'll experience while prepping for your next project.

I bet you've noticed that as an entrepreneur you're exceptional at generating new and innovative ideas. Yes, entrepreneurs are hard-wired for brilliance. Possibly because of this brilliance, *the three biggest challenges most entrepreneurs face:*

✓ Managing distractions

✓ Staying focused

✓ Making sure we have a handle on time and priorities

To that end, let's set you up with a toolbox that contains a few online and "old-fashioned" brilliance-organizing tools to help you capture your ideas and keep them organized in a way that makes them more accessible and easier to use in planning your next project.

Map it out!

A favorite mind-mapping tool that I've been using for years is Freemind. This versatile planning and time-management resource helps you put ideas into a map that allows you to quickly organize information in ways that make the most sense to you. In other words, it saves a lot of time by getting everything out of your head and into an easily accessible mind-map. I also recommend *Discover Freemind* (www.LeapWithoutLimits.com/mindmaptool), an easy-to-use, low-cost mind-mapping tutorial that includes installation, quick start, and advanced strategy videos on how to use the free Freemind software.

Gather your thoughts

Evernote, my favorite online tool, keeps my projects and business organized. Who wants to spend hours looking through hand-written and off-line tablet notes to find "important" information that you put in a "safe" place just the other day?

Evernote takes care of it all! You can add your ideas as text notes and clip and paste sections of reports or articles into a "note" that you can reference later, as well as quickly record an audio note to describe a web clip or new idea.

It's all there—access to everything in one location—wherever you are. All your ideas, notes, web clips, files, and images are kept in sync and made available on every mobile device and computer you use.

Find things in Evernote by simply searching by keyword or tag, and even printed and handwritten text inside images will pop up almost instantly to save you a lot of time.

And remember to share the brilliance. Evernote makes it a snap to share notes with team members, colleagues, and joint venture partners.

Put pen (or pencil) to paper

There's something *"special"* about putting pen to paper. Sure, you can keep track of your brilliance on a tablet or computer or through online tools. However, I discovered several years ago that a big part of my creative process is to doodle and write ideas and key concepts in an artist's sketchbook. A sketchbook seems to elevate the project and infuse a sense of art to the work in progress. I use colored gel pens whenever a new project is about to be born, and this creative act fuels inspiration *every time*! Here are some items to have on hand to capture and organize your brilliance:

1. An artist's sketchbook (add colored pens or pencils for "extra" flair)—Create the roadmap for your event with a sketchbook. There's something magical about a blank sheet of paper and the birth of a new project.

As you casually flip through your favorite magazines, notice images, design elements, and colors that speak to your creative side. Clip magazine images and create a collage in your sketchbook. This may be the inspiration you need to write your sales copy for your next product, service, or event (see Way 11: Magnetic Message).

2. A small notepad—Keep it nearby for bright ideas, action items, resources, and notes.

3. A three-ring binder with pocket dividers— A hard copy is just what's needed to refresh the memory of brilliance. Here are a few ways to use your three ring binder to design, plan, and organize your next project:

- ✓ Save favorite flyers from events you've attended. Notice the elements that speak to you. How can you integrate them into your work?

- ✓ Include a section for each workshop and class you teach and add your own notes. Identify what worked, what didn't, and what you'd do differently next time.

- ✓ Keep your Statement of Intent for the event in your binder (see Way 1: Create An Experience).

Create a new binder for each event (or project). In addition to placing the Statement of Intent in your binder, chronicle the steps you take along the way. It's easier to document the process as you go along. Include sections for inspiration, notes, sales copy, your templates, resources, and any other documentation that supports your work. This binder will serve as a valuable resource for your next event or project.

Bonus tips to capture and organize brilliance

Use the recorder on your cell phone as an audio notepad to record golden nuggets, flashes of brilliance, and reminders. Use video to get the word out about your event. Give us a sneak preview. Tell us briefly what you're up to way before the actual event. Record several short "spontaneous" videos and share them on your blog and through social media. It's another great way for your audience to get to know you, sense your level of excitement, and want to be part of it!

Resources in this Way:

 Discover Freemind:

 Evernote

R&R . . . Reflection and Relaxation

Projects come in all shapes and sizes, yet overall they require a ton of mental and emotional energy to come to fruition. There's an *intense* attention to detail that, if sustained for an extended period without an R&R outlet, can produce scattered or fragmented energy. To be fully energized and "all together" throughout the entire process while planning, implementing, and overseeing your project, it's vital to consistently include R&R—reflection and relaxation—in your routine!

Instant benefits

Regularly employ R&R each day to experience an increase in clear, focused, and creative energy that results in greater prosperity and a priceless physical payback of improved health and overall well-being.

Basics to achieve R&R:

Reflection helps us grow and make course corrections before they become overwhelming.

Reflection Exercise

Pause and engage in this reflective practice daily—during planning, implementation, and project oversight. You may want to capture your brilliance (see Way 3) for additional insights.

Notice what works! Say thank you often. Gratitude goes a long way for creating additional successes—both large and small (see Way 7).

What is not working? What can be done differently? When you have a lot going on, *pause*—take time to tune in to what's happening (but don't become too emotional) and map out a plan!

Feeling stuck? Wondering what comes next? Experience new possibilities by staying open to a shift in perspective during reflection.

Need additional support beyond team members? Oftentimes friends and colleagues will enthusiastically jump in to help out during crunch time or a challenge. The key is to ask.

"Free up" your mind. Write down or record ah-has, open items, and ideas that pop into your mind. Get information out of your head and to a place where you can quickly reference it whenever you need it (see Freemind and Evernote tips in Way 3).

Relaxation allows creative juices to flow and new opportunities to blossom naturally with more aliveness in each moment. Give yourself a gift—some quiet time every day!

You've been stretching yourself—planning and completing implementation milestones to produce a successful project. When was the last time you gave yourself permission to put your feet up and relax? Yep, that means doing *nothing,* even if it's only for five minutes a day. In this fast-paced race to get everything done before the "big day," it's essential to slow down and honor yourself. Your body needs it and your soul craves it. The practice of extreme self-care—developing daily habits that make you feel happy and nurtured—is a non-negotiable item on your way to thriving and becoming a prosperous entrepreneur.

Take time to just "be." Allow space for creative ideas to pop in. Go ahead, put your feet up and relax today—*at least for a few minutes*! Make this part of your extreme self-care practice and you'll notice that creative flow becomes more available to you. Have fun with it!

Dale Carnegie, a pioneer in public speaking and personal development, made a statement years ago that still rings true today: "People rarely succeed unless they have fun in what they're doing." Both reflection and relaxation can help you recapture the fun in planning and implementing a project by recharging and reviving your creative juices.

WAY 5

How to Keep from Being Overwhelmed

Even for the most organized individual, starting a new project or planning an event seems to send a high-alert signal to the universe. Hurry up; read this copy; wait, do that later; come over here; quick, create this; no wait, finish this first; pick this up; etc. "Excess" information has a way of taking on a life of its own. Face it: Busyness can be an energy zapper!

The physical, emotional, and mental sensory overload can quickly stop us in our tracks. The most debilitating part of feeling overwhelmed is the resulting constriction of creative juices and internal drive. It's thinking about all the things that need to be accomplished and wondering how in the world you're going to pull it off. A key to overcoming that overwhelmed feeling is to ***stop*** and acknowledge that you're over the top. According to Herbert Benson, M.D., in his book *The Relaxation Response*, this acknowledgement immediately sends signals to your body to relieve stress. You can turn that mental Ferris wheel and emotional roller coaster into something that is manageable, more productive, and much easier on your overall well-being. Ready to go for it? Start with these three basic steps:

Step 1: Remember to breathe

One of the quickest and easiest ways to overcome stress is to ***stop*** whatever you're doing and breathe consciously. You've been doing it all your life (breathing, that is); now put more awareness to it. Conscious breathing is about paying attention to the breath. Slowly inhale through the nose, hold for about three seconds, exhale slowly through the mouth, and feel your breath flow through your entire body—all the way to your toes. Repeat this at least three times. Conscious breathing quiets the mind, relaxes the body, and disengages the emotions. When the mind is relaxed, it's more expansive and clear. You can again engage your creativity.

The expression "stop and smell the roses" is a wonderful reminder to slow down and breathe in the essence of life.

Step 2: Be present or grounded in the here and now!

Grounding is rooted in stability. Now that you've mastered breathing, you're ready to ground yourself—to be present to whatever is happening *in the moment*. Think of a tree. The roots are planted in the earth, and even during a storm the tree has the ability to move, bend, and sway while remaining firmly planted in the ground. To ground yourself, stand tall and picture your head touching the sky. Breathe consciously through your body and feel your feet touching the earth. Be present. Sense your connection to the earth through the bottom of your feet. Continue this practice for at least three minutes.

Bonus Tip: This is a great centering technique to use while sitting at your desk or to relax at the end of the day.

Apply the grounding technique to help you experience a sense of peace. Being grounded brings in greater clarity about the present moment. The present moment naturally opens your mind to "bigger picture" thinking and allows new ideas or solutions to pop in.

Step 3: Slow down to speed up

Slowing down to speed up may sound counter-intuitive, yet it works! It's like having your own magic button that stops time in order for you to catch up, reorganize, and regain focus on what's important. The action steps seem to fall into place once you slow down.

Allow your creative genius to flow (*yes*, you have it) and assist you in identifying priorities and creating an action plan. Get out paper, colored pens and highlighters to create a list or mind map. It's important to get everything out of your mind, off tiny scraps of paper, and in one place. Once you've created your list of "projects," outline the steps and identify items that need to be addressed immediately. Add completion dates and use color codes to prioritize. You're almost there. Here's an important practice: Tune into what you want the outcome to look and feel like. In your mind, picture everything being completed with ease. After all, that's how you want it, right? Move forward confidently knowing you've got a plan that will take you to the finish line!

Resources in this Way:

 My *free* Overcome Overwhelm Toolkit that includes additional tips

Creative Energy

Have you noticed that when children discover something new, their whole being proclaims the revelation? That's creative energy at play. A child's eyes light up, the face brightens, the mouth opens wide, and there's a bubbly sense of excitement in the air. Wow—creation has revealed itself! The energy field surrounding this moment is electrifying, dynamic, and palpable.

Inside every human being, young and old, is an unseen, but very real, link to the source of all ideas. The link is easily accessible and readily available to provide information and creative ideas. A direct connection taps into the source of all creation and knowledge, past, present, and future.

Upon close examination of the idea that you can tap into your creative center, there's a realization and excitement that something big is taking place. (Excitement fuels creative energy!) This unseen process directly links the human mind with the Divine or the Universal Mind to bring into existence inspired, creative, innovative, and imaginative ideas. These ideas have the power to create innovation, as well as provide practical solutions to improve the quality of everyday life.

Let's examine the possibility of living a creatively inspired life by design. Put another way, to *consciously* create a life that fulfills your destiny and is light years beyond your wildest dream. What if the Universe provided each of us with a gift? The gift card says, "In each moment, you have the ability to start over—to begin again and re-create a spectacular life for yourself. Simply begin dreaming and through intent (see Way 1) consciously create each new experience."

If you're ready to break through the limitations that are holding you back, step outside your current belief system for a brief moment. Picture a world where individuals get excited about a life filled with adventure, exploration, and discovery instead of *worrying* about health care, child care, lack of time, lackluster careers, and paying the bills. **Stop!!** Stop for a moment. All it takes is one *good* creative idea to surface into your conscious mind, and you're on your way to greatly improving your life and hopefully the lives of others. Now that's something to get excited about!

A Touch of G-Force

How often do you tap into G-Force: gratitude and grace to fuel your business projects and life? When you've got this powerful pair pulling for you, you're able to move forward with more ease, and you frequently experience synchronistic opportunities that take your business and life to new heights.

It's important to be grateful for what you have in your life and business, as this action attracts more of it to you. What you may not know is that grace and gratitude seem to always appear in concert. When you take the time to observe, acknowledge, recognize, and *appreciate what "is,"* the energy of gratitude calls in grace.

Have you ever had a time in your life when things came together easily and effortlessly? It may have felt as if the details were being taken care of behind the scenes and all you had to do was show up. That's grace at work!

The energy of grace is available to each of us at any given moment. Grace is an assisting energy that steps in at the perfect time, with the perfect solution, and just the right resources. It's particularly helpful to call upon grace when you're in need of divine intervention—you know, those times when everything seems off. The elegance of grace allows us to be in touch with all that is—the abundance of life!

Express your gratitude by connecting with the feeling and being thankful for things you may take for granted: your senses, a restful night, your ears that hear, your voice that enables you to express yourself and communicate with others, the sun, the flowers, hot and cold running water, the mountains, a comfy chair to relax in and watch your favorite show, etc. The more deliberate you are in the practice of expressing gratitude, the more grace and ease show up to assist you in the everyday.

Let's do a quick *G-Force Experience*

An easy way to activate more grace in your business and life is to put pen to paper. Take out a journal or sheet of paper and write down five things you're grateful for in your business and another five things you're grateful for in your life. Continue this practice daily for at least sixty days and watch what happens.

With the powerful duo of gratitude and grace working for you, even major missteps can be resolved in record time. This potent partnership helps you to wake up and pay attention to the signs, symbols, and messages that lead to a richer, more fulfilling, and success-filled business and life. This partnership allows you to see the meaning and purpose behind what at first appear to be random, everyday events that are, in fact, signposts that guide and direct you to experience life fully. *Let the G-Force be with you!!*

Aligned for Greater Prosperity

As an entrepreneur, how often is your energy tugged on and pulled in various directions? If you're like most entrepreneurs, your mind rarely rests and there's a tendency to work long hours with a persistent drive to innovate and improve results. It's no wonder you may feel stressed and stretched to the max. From an energetic perspective, your fuel gauge is reading empty and you're operating on vapors in overdrive. Time out. There is a "new" way to actualize your desires and achieve success. Now is the ideal time to break through your limits to bring "new" energy and exciting opportunities into your business. Get recharged with an energy alignment session.

For more than a decade, I've had the honor as a naturally gifted and professionally trained healer to work with individuals and groups to align their energy. What initially started as health-related alignments swiftly evolved to successfully aligning desired business outcomes with performances to match! The silver lining to each alignment is when individuals consistently feel more centered and relaxed, the more able they are to create the successful results they're looking for. Now that's a resounding **Y.E.S.** (Way 16) that accelerates prosperity and success!

Alignment Basics

You have four bodies. Yes, you read that right, four energy bodies—a physical body, an emotional body, a mental body, and a spiritual body—that are constantly communicating with each other.

From a communication and well-being perspective, there's a lot going on in the subtle or invisible energy field of the four bodies that determines overall performance and results in your business and life. Here's a dynamic that's food for thought: Let's say the emotional body craves cake, the mental body doesn't want the cake, the physical body can't digest the cake, and the spiritual body desires your highest good. You've got a lot of mixed energetic signals or messages between the bodies that create confusion and prevent you from being the most miraculous version of you.

An energetic alignment creates harmony and peace among the physical, emotional, mental, and spiritual energy bodies so the four bodies work together as a team toward the same goal and result. An alignment session can be done in person or over the phone and is able to quickly shift and adjust energy to get you laser focused on next steps that will move you forward.

An energy alignment is able to accomplish magical things:

- ✓ Calls in scattered energy
- ✓ Creates an inner awareness that signals the creative genius within the four bodies to speak to each other
- ✓ Facilitates clear communication
- ✓ Brings understanding and cooperation to all your bodies
- ✓ Enables you to "feel" and "act" in accordance with your desires

Typical "physical" alignment benefits:

- ✓ Increased physical relaxation

- ✓ Greater peace of mind
- ✓ A centered, balanced feeling
- ✓ Restful sleep
- ✓ An excitement about moving forward
- ✓ Clarity about next steps
- ✓ The decision and inspired action to make "it" happen

When aligned, you're operating at a higher frequency and working with a creative impulse that draws to you higher "vibrating" results—greater prosperity with more grace and ease (Way 7). What if being prosperous is really about a steady flow of support—materially, emotionally, intellectually, and spiritually?

Reach for high aspirations. Subscribing to the belief that there is more than enough prosperity to go around is actually an invitation to create the sensation. Being in alignment with this belief produces a self-fulfilling actualization!

Resources in this Way:

 LeapWithoutLimits.com/Align

When It Almost Doesn't Happen

Let's say you've been putting a lot of resources into a "dream" project or an event, and you hit a major snag. What do you do? If you've been applying the law of attraction (which simply states you attract into your life whatever you think about), to your "dream" and still waiting for the big reveal, would you be interested in speeding up the process? It's time to use an energetic approach to creation. When your subtle energy (see Way 16) lines up around creating what you want (better relationships, overall health, abundance, more energy), the 5-D or multi-dimensional approach works every time. You can thrive in all areas of your life!

Each 5-D element is fueled by the energy of inspiration:

- ✓ **D**ream—the "what" you want to be, do, have, or share

- ✓ **D**esire—the driver of your dream

- ✓ **D**ecision—a conscious choice to move forward—you're going for it

- ✓ **D**esign—imagine what "it" looks and feels like

- ✓ **D**o—take inspired action

Looking for simple solutions and radical results? Ride the wave of inspiration (see Way 2). The following story guides you through the elements of this 5-D approach.

Based on my experience with clients in seeing what would help them achieve their heart's desire or goals, I told my business coach and mastermind partners that I would like to create my own deck of inspirational cards. Before I knew it, I made a commitment to create a deck of cards *and* a companion book within three months. The **Dream** and **Desire** elements of creation were set in motion.

The more I thought about creating the cards, the more excited I became. The more excited

I became, the easier it was to move forward. G-Force (see Way 7) was definitely at play. With the support of inner guidance, the **Decision** (third element of creation) was a natural next step. My inner guidance, a trusted friend, said, "*Do it!* It will be a leaping point for you and your clients."

The project progressed smoothly until logistics caused everything to come to a screeching halt. For almost a week, I went back and forth with various printers outlining the requirements (size, card stock, finish, etc.) in order to establish project estimates. Much to my disappointment, every production estimate was astronomical. Plus, we still needed to add printing costs for the companion guide into the mix. It looked like the card project wasn't going to happen. I *almost* gave up and let go of the idea.

What happened next was magical. Whenever I run up against obstacles in life, I immediately employ the following three secret creation elements:

Visualize the desired outcome—put clear focused attention and energy into what the end result "*looks*" and "feels" like.

Let go—become unattached. *Stop pushing or pulling it forward. And, most importantly...*

Trust—that if it's meant to be, the result will happen!

I encourage you to give the three secret creation elements a go when you're stuck. The results can be astounding. In my case, I wanted (and imagined receiving) a reasonable price quote that met the card specifications, accelerated timeline, and included the printing cost for the companion guidebook.

It only took two days to experience the desired results. Without any prompting on my part, the name of a new printer who met all the requirements made its way to me. Yes, the project was back on track. I love when this happens!

The thirty-three Just **BE** . . . Boundless Energy Cards were **designed for self-discovery and transformation**. Each card features a photograph from my personal travels paired with a specific word to help you discover a rich moment of inspiration. To assist with transformation while using the cards, each card was infused with a specific energy during the design phase.

The cards went into production and it looked like the entire card project (including guidebook) would meet the original three-month schedule. This was great news.

It looked like the finished cards would be available to showcase at my friend's upcoming event . . . until, it almost didn't happen!

The printer informed me of minor production issues that he said would quickly be resolved. A week later, there was still a problem with one card that kept holding up the production run. My friend's event was two days away and I needed at least one sample deck for the guests. Knowing the urgency, the printer sent the proof deck overnight and warned me that the *"problem card"* was in the deck. He reassured me, "Don't worry, we fixed the card and everything is running smoothly."

I couldn't wait for the mail. As I flipped through the deck, I immediately spotted the card that resembled the original, but was different. I laughed and cried as I looked at the **Transform** card—it literally transformed itself in production. In the **Transform** proof image the once beautiful orange and red leaves on the ground and on the lower branches of the tree transformed themselves into green leaves. What a powerful validation for the fourth element in creation, **Design**—imagining the look and feel of the end result. To this day, it's still a mystery to the printer as to why the Transform card transformed itself during production. To order your own deck of these transformational cards visit LeapWithoutLimits.com/be.

Resources in this Way:

 Just **BE** . . . **Boundless** Energy Cards

WAY 10

Tune In to Intuition

It's been known by many names. Some call it a hunch, an ah-ha, a notion, a vibe, an instinct, a wonder, and even an inkling, just to name a few. Regardless of how you refer to intuition, it's here to assist you in every day situations. Intuition is often subtle, yet it can have a huge impact on the outcome—especially during an event.

An intuitive flash comes quickly, often out of nowhere without your logical mind being involved. For many, building intuitive confidence takes practice. Begin by listening to and embracing intuition as your best friend. Write down the intuitive hunches or inklings you receive, even if they're subtle and you'd be inclined to ignore them. The more affirming evidence you gather about your intuitive "hits," the more trusting and responsive you become to the information.

Employ intuition—a very natural business talent

Successful entrepreneurs, presenters, and planners know that a major contributor to event success is knowing "how" to read the event (i.e., what's really happening) and respond quickly to change things on the fly. Here's where intuition comes in handy. Be open to intuitive nudges and ask for them ahead of time. Then expect to receive information that will guide you to the next steps.

Let's say it's the *big* day of your live event. You're confidently stepping on stage to give your presentation. You've prepared and practiced your content and know your "easy yes" offer inside and out. Be open to intuitive information on the fly during your presentation to assist with unknown circumstances and questions that may arise. Take cues from the audience. The body language and facial expressions of audience members provide valuable hints about understanding, comfort levels, and overall interest.

Make **S.P.A.** moments a part of your presentation. Anytime I think or say "spa" it brings a happy relaxed feeling to mind and an image of being pampered in a luxury setting. Ahhhhh. **S.P.A.** moments: **S**top, **P**ause, and **A**llow your intuition to guide you whenever you notice a need to shift perspective or change directions.

The more you tune in to your intuition—a direct link to higher brilliance—the easier it is to receive new information, shift gears, and experience new possibilities. Here's to experiencing out-of-this-world event performance and prosperity!

Magnetic Message

Want more impact with your message? Whether it's sales copy, marketing information, a project presentation, or a conversation with a potential client, words that are spoken (and written) from the heart have a significantly greater magnetic attraction than those coming from just your mind. There's even science behind it.

Studies by the Institute of HeartMath, a nonprofit research organization, have shown that *the electrical* strength of the heart's signal, measured by an electrocardiogram (EKG), is up to *sixty times as great* as the electrical signal from the human brain, measured by an electroencephalogram (EEG). Here's the WOW part: *The heart's magnetic field* is *as much as 5,000 times stronger than that of the brain.* What's important here is that either field has the power to magnify our messages, and we create both whenever we communicate!

When we consciously form heart-based messages that we truly believe, we're creating the electrical and magnetic expression of them as energy. These invisible waves of energy, which aren't confined to our hearts or limited by the physical barrier of our skin and bones, are "speaking" to the world around us in each moment of every day through a language that has no words—the belief waves of our hearts. Now that's powerful messaging!

Let's say your desire is to create a marketing message to attract the "right" people to show up as participants at an upcoming new product presentation. Here are five steps to magnify and magnetize your message:

Step 1: Heart-based answers form the basis of your message

Be in your heart while outlining the answers to the following questions:

- ✓ Who is my audience?

- ✓ What is their major challenge? or What am I inspiring them to do?

- ✓ Why do they have this challenge?
- ✓ What do they need?
- ✓ What are my solutions to their needs?

Step 2: Identify the compelling message

Using the answers from Step 1, identify your compelling message. An example of a compelling key message for a recent presentation directed toward speakers, authors, coaches, consultants, and service professionals who are unsatisfied with their current sales results reads: "Discover Powerful Y.E.S. Sales Secrets. Energize Your Sales. Get More Clients and Be Prosperous!"

Step 3: Begin the energetic process

Bring your attention to the here and now by clearing your mind of any thoughts that keep you from being present. Take in three deep clearing breathes.

Step 4: Read out loud

Read the compelling key message you created in Step 2 out loud three times to create a key magnetic message. Put heart into it. Magnetize it—really feel the words and what they can do for your audience as you say them!

Step 5: Energetically extend an invitation to your ideal audience

Use your imagination. See yourself energetically connecting and greeting your guests—shaking hands or giving them a hug. Be sure to extend a heartfelt welcome.

Through your magnetic message, you're on your way to creating greater prosperity by connecting with your ideal audience and potential clients.

Bonus Tip: Craft and lay out your magnetic message (online sales copy) in WordPress quickly and easily using Premise, *my favorite* WordPress resource. Premise allows you to create multiple types of professional landing pages, without using code. Premise also has many features, including custom graphics and sample copywriting templates, which make crafting your magnetic message a snap!

Resources in this Way:

 LeapWithoutLimits.com/ Premise

WAY 12

Super Easy and Natural Success

Super success is a natural extension of consistently applying practices that move you in alignment with your intent (see Way 1). Then, it's up to you to take action. We all have the potential to be magnificent and successful. Whenever we resonate and fully embody a value or belief that's "true" for us, it's like flipping the "on" switch and supercharging our success.

The fifteen super success tips found below have the power to energetically uplift you and your level of success. Read each tip out loud and place extra emphasis on the italicized words.

To stay on the success track, implement a morning and evening practice or "ritual" that becomes a natural part of your day. I recommend you identify one or two statements that you most want to integrate into your life on a monthly basis. For the next thirty days, every morning when you wake up and evening before you close your eyes, use the statement as a mantra to affirm what is currently in your life or your desire for more of it to show up. For example, Success Tip No. 1 becomes the following mantra, "I am bolder than I have ever been before." It's great for building confidence and stretching your comfort zone.

Enjoy these fifteen super success tips and be sure to make them your own:

- ✓ *Be bolder* than you've ever been before.

- ✓ Look at *all* your *knowledge* as a *valuable gift* you get to *share* with others.

- ✓ Always *be gentle and kind to yourself,* even when you mess up.

- ✓ Be *generous* with your wisdom.

- ✓ *Smile* at strangers!

- ✓ See the *extra*ordinary in the ordinary—look for the *light* in all things.

- ✓ *Give yourself permission* to do "nothing" for at least five minutes each day.

- ✓ Take time every day to fully take in a *loving thought* about you!

- ✓ Express *appreciation* often!

- ✓ Ensure that your daily schedule *reflects* your *deepest values*.

- ✓ Sense what brings you *joy*! *Listen* with your heart.

- ✓ *Transcend F.E.A.R.*—**F**alse **E**vidence **A**ppearing **R**eal!

- ✓ Learn something new *every day*.

- ✓ Upon waking each morning ask yourself, "How can I *best serve* the most people?"

- ✓ *Celebrate* small successes and unleash a huge amount of *momentum* and positive energy.

As you practice and integrate these success tips into your day, you're investing time and energy in building success muscles for your business and life.

WAY 13

Authentic Self-expression

How often do you allow yourself to fully express who you are to the outside world? If your tendency is to hold back the "real" authentic you, do you realize it takes more energy to hold back than to let go and be you? The expression, "Be yourself—all others are taken," speaks directly to allowing your uniqueness to come through.

Art Linkletter, a friend and colleague of Walt Disney, wrote the foreword to Pat Williams' book *How to Be Like Walt*. In this foreword, Linkletter shares Walt Disney's most endearing qualities worth emulating—his optimism, integrity, courage, imagination, creativity, leadership, boldness, perseverance, and commitment to excellence—just to name a few.

Linkletter was asked what Disney might think and say about a book called *How to Be Like Walt.* Knowing his friend as well as he did, Linkletter felt Disney might not like the book title at all. In fact, Disney would probably lift an eyebrow and make a statement about the importance of everyone being himself or herself instead of like him or anyone else.

The more you allow yourself to fully express who you are to the outside world, the easier it is for individuals to get to know you. And you know what that means: The quicker people get to like and trust you, the faster they say yes to working with you.

Sure, it takes courage to stay faithful and true to our values—our internal, rather than external, influences. Authentic self-expression is dynamic energy that portrays feeling, spirit, or character. Instead of being a facsimile of someone else, you're able to allow your unique essence to come through.

Bring your authentic self to all that you do. Connect with that part of you that's magnificent to discover your uniqueness and let your colors shine. Your power is in walking your talk. Don't save it or hide it. Give it away. You're here to share your gift and change people's lives!

Flo Aeveia Magdalena, author of *Sunlight on Water* and *I Remember Union,* has some inspiring words on the subject of personal authenticity. "There is a space for you in the world with your name on it," she says, "and your part is the lead part. No matter who you are, it's the lead. Because only you can play it, and without you it doesn't happen."

Notice what comes naturally for you and then embrace and expand this expression. It's safe to stretch your boundaries and comfort zone when it's in alignment (see Ways 8 and 16) with who you are. Your purpose is far greater than you can even imagine. Go ahead and unleash your authentic self-expression—we're ready to applaud you and your message!

Journey

Planning an event is much like planning a wedding. It's a journey with a great destination. For the host of a live event, there are many things to keep in mind:

- ✓ Selecting and securing the "ideal" date
- ✓ A great venue
- ✓ Meeting and breakout rooms that meet your needs
- ✓ Accommodations for out-of-town attendees
- ✓ Food and beverage
- ✓ Technology set-up

Ideally, you leave the site negotiations and planning details in the capable hands of an event planner. This gives you time to focus on content and creating the event experience (Way 1). To assist your team with logistical matters, download a free event-planning checklist at: LeapWithoutLimits.com/event-checklist.

Once you identify the destination (see Way 1 – Create an Experience) and are clear minded about the direction, let the journey begin. Cultivate a sense of awe and wonder about this adventure. It will lead you to higher potential and greater prosperity. Wake up each morning bright-eyed and ready to experience the opportunities before you. Be open and get excited about synchronicities that appear out of nowhere and make the journey smoother. Let's face it, sometimes opportunities wear a mask and are disguised as setbacks. Instead of "stopping dead in your tracks," simply use your ability to discern what's meant to be by tuning into your internal guidance system—also known as intuition (see Way 10).

Remember, there is no one in the world like *you*. You are a fabulous, awe-inspiring person who's initiating a journey. When you get excited about your event, others can feel the excitement and they'll want to join in the adventure.

The key element that you are completely in charge of on this journey is *you!* What influences your event more than anything else is how you think and feel about it! Let's repeat this one more time. You have direct control over how you'd like to experience the event. This in turn is energetically broadcast to attendees and impacts how the audience "picks up" the event.

In fact, what you think about and feel about a variety of events and occurrences in your life directly reflects the way you experience them. If you wake each morning thinking, "Oh, it's just another same-old, same-old day," you'll get the same kind of day over and over again (remember the movie, *Groundhog Day*). You, however, are on a journey. Get ready to explore another approach and experience something different. Begin now to expect great movement in your life.

What kind of event do you yearn to create?

Is it a one-, two-, or three-day creative adventure filled with great content from multiple speakers that empower and inspire your audience to impact more people?

Perhaps you've always wanted to bring your VIP clients to a three-day renewal retreat at a luxury resort!

Or, maybe you want to host a two-hour "How to" workshop for your local garden club.

Rest assured that what you want to create can be created. Identifying the "what wants to be created" is the first step. Unsure what type of event resonates with you for your attendees? Use your creative imagination to explore the journey first, get aligned (Way 8) with the vision, and then take inspired action whenever necessary. Go ahead, step on the path and let the exploration begin.

Resources in this Way:

 Free Event Planning Checklist and another special offer from Workshop and Seminar Expert, Daphne Bousquet

Focus

Where would you like to focus your time and energy? Whether it's writing a book, creating a new product, developing a train-the-trainer program, or whatever your project is, it's very likely that things are piling up on your "to-do" list, and they need attention. There's a saying, "Your energy will flow where your attention goes."

If your attention is focused on simultaneously jumping and racing through multiple "to-dos" that are tugging on you, your energy becomes fragmented. In other words, your energy reaches and stretches in many directions—much like the arms of a starfish. To maximize time and energy, you must be completely present and focused on one project or activity at a time.

For many of us, the "ticking clock" and looming deadlines to be met lead to ineffective work and procrastination. If you experience a high number of distractions and interruptions during the day that keep your motivation and focus low, here is a simple solution that will help.

The Pomodoro Technique, an easy-to-apply and highly effective time-management technique, was created by Francesco Cirillo (see PomodoroTechnique.com). By using a simple tool and a five-step process, this technique improves productivity and enhances focus and concentration by cutting down on interruptions. As an added energy bonus, the Pomodoro Technique moves you forward, elevates your personal effectiveness, and alleviates angst linked to the myriad of "to-dos" on your list.

The technique uses a timer to break down periods of work into twenty-five-minute intervals called "pomodoros," separated by breaks. The method is based on the idea that frequent breaks can improve mental agility. (If you're wondering why the term "pomodoro" is used for the twenty-five-minute intervals, Cirillo, the creator of this technique, used a kitchen timer shaped like a *pomodoro*—the Italian word for tomato.) The Pomodoro Technique includes five basic steps:

Step 1

Decide on the task to be done

Step 2

Set the pomodoro—the timer—to twenty-five minutes

Step 3

Work on the task until the *timer rings*

Step 4

Take a short five-minute break. (If you have a tendency to take longer breaks, you may want to use the timer for your five-minute break.)

Step 5

After every four "pomodoros," take a longer break (fifteen to twenty minutes)

The energy of *focus* is laser-like—clear and purposeful. When you're clear about what it is you would like to accomplish and take consistent action steps, you'll quickly get more done and feel more relaxed, too.

Resources in this Way:

 The Pomodoro Technique

WAY 16

A Resounding Y.E.S.

Civil rights leader Mahatma Gandhi gives a definition of greatness that intrigues me: "As human beings, our greatness lies not so much in being able to remake the world . . . as in being able to remake ourselves." This is central to the next Way I will discuss, *Y.E.S.*

From an energetic level, there's so much more to you than your physical body. ***Y.E.S.** stands for **Y**our **E**nergetic **S**ignal. **Y**our **E**nergetic **S**ignal* is a vibration—the "real" you—and it's constantly transmitting and communicating who you are to your audience, potential clients, and the world. Before they get to know, like, and trust you, your "audience" is receiving "hidden signals," or an energetic hint, about you and your business. This means we're always conveying our brand message—even before we write sales copy or utter a single word.

Five secrets to energize results and create greater prosperity

You are more than your physical body. Energetically, you have four bodies, each with its own rate of vibration. You have a physical body, an emotional body, a mental body, and a spiritual body that continually communicate with each other and the world around you.

Your Energetic Signal, a "composite" vibration representing all four of your energy bodies, reflects your purpose, thoughts, feelings, and actions to create the primary vibration of your being. This fundamental vibration then creates resonance with identical vibration frequencies in the universe and draws them for you to experience.

Yes, we attract circumstances, people, challenges, and opportunities that resonate with our own dominant vibration frequency.

You can discover your vibration frequency by becoming an observer of yourself. Pay attention to your thoughts, feelings, and actions and the resulting experiences. For the record, *Your*

E*nergetic **S**ignal* is outcome neutral. The experience or reality you call in always matches the energy signal you send out.

If you're feeling stuck or unfulfilled and experiencing less than stellar results in your business and life, notice if your thoughts, feelings, and actions reflect one of the following:

- ✓ Judgment of self, others, and situations
- ✓ Attachment to an outcome
- ✓ Resistance to what is

By dwelling on, complaining about, whining about, worrying about, fearing, judging, criticizing, and resisting what's currently happening in your business and life, you automatically create "lower" vibration experiences. And you will continue to create situations that hold this exact same vibration until you take responsibility and internally shift your energy.

A simple and elegant way to increase the frequency and number of higher vibrating experiences is to align the energy of all four bodies so they communicate and resonate with each other.

To align with the creative power of the universe around you, invite the best friend energies of acceptance, enjoyment, and enthusiasm to be part of your inner circle. Be consistent and persistent in playing with the energies of acceptance, enjoyment, and enthusiasm daily. Before very long, you'll feel different and you'll energetically be different—attracting more life magic into your everyday experience.

Resources in this Way:

 LeapWithoutLimits.com/Align

Accelerate your success. Y.E.S., when Your Energetic Signal is fully aligned, your confidence increases, resulting in peak performance and greater prosperity.

Align Your Energetic Signal so potential clients consistently say, "Yes!"

WAY 17

Emerge and Become Visible

To become known for your work and genius, you must show up and become visible. You are incredible in so many ways. Look at yourself, blossoming with gifts and talents that are uniquely yours. Allow your brilliance to shine forth for the world to see. You've got tremendous value to showcase and it's time to emerge, instead of being the best-kept secret!

If you're waiting to publish a book or launch another project until you've reached your ideal weight, have the perfect website, or a myriad of other reasons before you allow yourself to become visible, you're delaying getting your work into the world. The time is now and the key is to take baby steps every day. Be persistent and consistent in showing up and adding value. Pretty soon, you'll look back and realize you've grown by leaps and bounds. Here are three simple steps to becoming visible:

Step 1: Connect

As you're *emerging with your gifts*, it's essential that you build relationships—both locally and globally. And these relationships should add value to the lives of those you connect with. Several years ago, American author and poet Maya Angelou spoke at a local event I attended. I'll always remember how she made us feel and her words of wisdom. "I've learned that people will forget what you said, people will forget what you did," she said, "but people will never forget how you made them feel."

To make people feel special, the whole idea is to connect. Allow others to get to know, like, and trust you. Every time you step out of your house, be the outgoing, genuine, and generous person you are and have always wanted to be more of. Say hello and smile, even to passersby. The simple act of greeting a person with warmth and an open heart acknowledges their presence and makes them feel like a VIP—a very important person who is pleased to make your acquaintance.

And there are many ways to build these connections. Thanks to social media, you can build relationships with people all over the world, even from the comfort of your home. Only a few short years ago, who would have thought that it would be just as easy (and sometimes easier) to build relationships half-way around the world as quickly as with your next door neighbor? Use these relationships to build a deep level of connection.

Step 2: Attend live events

Sure it's important to stay up to date with the latest developments in your industry, observe various hosting styles and presentation formats, and catch ideas for your own event. What's even more significant about attending a live event is the opportunity to network with like-minded individuals and instructors who are generous with their knowledge. Oftentimes, the people you meet at events turn out to be perfect joint venture partners, speakers, team members, and even potential sponsors who will support your future endeavors. You might even meet a client or two.

There is also something really wonderful about traveling to an out-of-town event. In addition to discovering new places it's so exciting to meet new people from outside of your immediate market. These new connections can give a fresh perspective that can inspire you to try something new.

You can also build your virtual network. One of the first things I do after attending a live event is to connect with other attendees online through Facebook, LinkedIn, and Twitter. Frequently, event hosts facilitate this process by setting up a special Facebook group to encourage attendees to continue the conversations and allow relationships to grow.

Stay open to possibilities. In addition to new friendships, many of the individuals I've met at live events have helped me emerge by cheering me on while showcasing and supporting my work!

Step 3: Come out of hiding

Allow your true self to shine. Now is not the time to be shy. Speak up. Tell family, friends, colleagues, and local and global buddies what you're up to. What's your calling? If you've always wanted to speak professionally, write a book, or create simple yet elegant retreats for overworked executives and don't know where to begin, get training and hire a coach or mentor to be your guide.

If you find yourself speaking in front of people both personally and professionally and want to be more confident and compelling, then be sure to pick up the free special report, *Be A Compelling Speaker* at LeapWithoutLimits.com/compellingspeaker. Whether you want to get your point across effectively at a sales presentation, during a meeting, or ask a question at an event, this report will help you excel in all speaking situations. You may also want to check out another book in this series, *21 Ways to Make Money Speaking* by speaking coach and professional Felicia Slattery, M.A., M.Ad.Ed.

Be true to yourself and your calling, even when obstacles appear in your path. Give yourself permission to trust your authentic self to reveal the magnificence of who you truly are. Keep going. Grow!! Before you know it, you will become the person you have always wanted to be.

Resources in this Way:

 *Be A Compelling Speaker,* a free special report by Caterina Rando, founder of The Sought-After Speaker Summit and The Business Breakthrough Summit

 *21 Ways to Make Money Speaking* by Felicia Slattery, M.A., M.Ad.Ed.

Begin

Today is a new day. How are you seeing the world as you wake up each morning? Realize the highest possibilities for your business and life by cultivating a sense of awe and wonder.

Have you ever watched a beautiful sunrise on water? It begins as a glistening beam of light and spreads in all directions. It's a spectacular sign for all to witness that a new day is being born.

Are you planning to add something "new" to your business and create greater prosperity for you and the people you serve? How often have you promised yourself that you'll begin _____ tomorrow? (You fill in the blank.) Well, the sun has risen and that tomorrow is now today, so stop waiting. Begin, *now!*

If the "bigness" of your mission is making you feel small, you want to break through your fear. Feel the F.E.A.R. (False Evidence Appearing Real), take a deep breath, and go for it. Leap! Trust you'll be given wings to fly or that a safety net will appear.

You have within you tremendous gifts and talents that the world is waiting for. It's the perfect time to set into motion your heart's desire and create that teleseminar series (LeapWithoutLimits.com/instant-teleseminar or FreeConferenceCalling.com), telesummit, or live event you've always dreamed of.

Sure it's a stretch to begin presenting—especially if you're new to presenting or are not extremely tech-savvy. The only way to get started is to begin.

Begin uncovering technology secrets

Initially, whenever I heard successful online entrepreneurs say, "Technology is not my thing," I often wondered how these entrepreneurs could successfully operate an online business without thoroughly understanding the ins and outs of technology. Once I learned their secret to success, I understood a deeper truth. Instead of spending mega hours mastering technology, savvy entrepreneurs *begin* by learning and understanding the technology basics. Then they hire a virtual assistant to oversee the technical areas and spend their time and energy on marketing, sales, and working with clients, as well as creating and delivering great content. There is nothing wrong with getting professional assistance to help boost your technological presence.

There are resources to help you along the way. If you're interested in creating a virtual event and are befuddled by the technology (and strategy) needed to host a teleseminar, then Bob The Teacher Jenkins is your go-to guy! Bob, a sought-after business coach, speaker, and Internet marketing consultant, makes the complex world of technology and online marketing simple. He connects big picture strategies with step-by-step tactics you need to succeed in creating your dream business. I can attest to this. Jenkins is the first "teacher" and business coach I turned to. I'm so grateful for his support in helping me Leap Without Limits. Learning from Bob is like first arriving in the Land of Oz—everything turns from black and white to full color! Visit LeapWithoutLimits.com/Bob for more details.

Resources for this Way:

 Instant Teleseminar

 FreeConferenceCalling.com

 Bob the Teacher Jenkins

WAY 19

A Stretch

Albert Einstein said it best, "There are only two ways to live your life. One is as though nothing is a miracle. The other is as though everything is a miracle." What would happen if you stretched your perspective to look for the miracle and beauty in everything?

Ready to leap without limits? Expansion, growth, and extending something beyond limits all come from stretching your perspective. You've probably heard the expression, "What you see is what you get!" Right? As you process what you "see," your reference system validates the experience. Here's where things become circular: The more you view things in the same way, the more things stay the same. As you begin to stretch your perspective, your business and life become richer and more dynamically alive.

Here are three go-to practices that cultivate a stretch in perspective everyday:

Open eyes

Look for the extraordinary in the ordinary! A fun way to keep your eyes "open" for new views is to do a little experimenting with a digital camera. When an image catches your eye, snap away, taking in different views. Zoom in, zoom out, step back, go around, and look at things from various angles. Oftentimes "hidden" treasures appear in the image after the pictures are taken. For example, I focused my camera on an unusual looking flower that I fell in love with and later I noticed that the background contained a heart-shaped stone. Wow, something that went unnoticed while taking the picture.

Conversations

Pay attention to your inner dialogue. Here's how it works: While doing whatever it is you're doing in life, pay attention to the conversation you're having in your mind. Tune in to your self-talk. Listen to the words you use and overall tone of your voice.

Is it uplifting and inspiring (moving you forward) or are you sliding on the slippery slope of self-sabotage by criticizing yourself and remaining stuck? Move forward quickly to experience a fuller, richer, more prosperous life by actively listening for and sanctioning uplifting inner conversations.

Feel the energy

Notice the energy around feelings. Feelings have a direct influence on perception. Take a moment and feel the energy of light-heartedness, playfulness, and excitement. What do you get? Now feel the energy of judgment, pain, or fear. Very different! As you gain experience in being fully present in each moment and tune in to the energy of what's going on in you, around you, and with others, you're developing super sensory skills that stretch your perspective and provide access to valuable knowledge.

WAY 20

From Ordinary to Extraordinary

Everyone can share his or her message with the world. Thanks to huge advances in teleseminar and webinar technology, you have the ability to reach out and touch many in the world without having to travel beyond your home office. Having extraordinary vision is no longer limited to a small circle or secret club. As a passion-filled leader, you can create the same visibility that was only possible for corporate giants just a few short years ago. This adventure is simultaneously scary and exciting. The path you've chosen awakens your sleeping giant and brings you into the power that is your birthright.

As writer Marianne Williamson says in *A Return to Love:* "Our deepest fear is not that we are inadequate. Our deepest fear is that we are powerful beyond measure. It is our light, not our darkness that most frightens us. We ask ourselves, 'Who am I to be brilliant, gorgeous, talented, fabulous?' Actually, who are you not to be?"

Recognize and acknowledge the "extra" that is already within you. Williamson continues, "Your playing small does not serve the world. There is nothing enlightened about shrinking so that other people won't feel insecure around you. We are all meant to shine, as children do. We were born to make manifest the glory of God that is within us. It's not just in some of us; it's in everyone. And as we let our own light shine, we unconsciously give other people permission to do the same. As we are liberated from our own fear, our presence automatically liberates others."

Give up playing small. Go for it—be *brilliant, gorgeous, talented,* and *fabulous!* You were born to play this role.

Remember, the decision to go bigger automatically connects you with the *extra* measures—*the inspired actions*—that create extraordinary experiences and outcomes for you and the people you serve.

The time is now. The more excited and confident you get about your vision, gifts, and talents, the quicker you fire up the electrifying energy that draws to you what you desire to experience in the first place. The world is waiting for you to inspire us to become greater than we've ever been before!

WAY 21

High-Vibe Service

Something amazing happens when your mission, purpose, and service (your "work" that's fueled by passion) align! You feel fully alive and know you're here to "play a much bigger role" in your "service" business. Although invisible to the naked eye, there's an elevated energy encircling high-vibe service providers.

High-vibe service providers resonate with the following characteristics and statements:

High-vibe service providers understand customers and clients are looking for an experience (see Way 1) that takes them on a journey (see Way 14), lifts them up, and returns them to the same place—fully charged ready to take the next step.

Clients who work with high-vibe service providers experience *profound* shifts and transformations, usually within a short timeframe.

Potential (energy match) clients find the magnetic message (see Way 11) of high-vibe service providers irresistible and are willing to pay handsomely for what they have to offer.

What's interesting about this magnetic energy is some individuals can put words to it, while others cannot. Yet, on some level, joint venture partners, sponsors, team members, and clients can feel it and are drawn to it.

High-vibe services have an innate desire to connect and work with individuals, businesses, and companies who consistently "walk the talk" and have the "it" qualities of *i*ntegrity and **t**rust.

- ✓ High-vibe service providers have a soul calling and are socially conscious.

- ✓ High-vibe service is about being in the zone (see Way 6) when you're doing what you love, and just as importantly when you're doing mundane things.

- ✓ High-vibe service providers know it's a *duty* or calling to make a difference and in doing so they are always *supported by a deep inner knowing* (see Way 10).

- ✓ High-vibe service providers want to make **big** systemic changes simply to *do good*.

- ✓ Make no mistake: High-vibe service providers are interested in financial gain; however, the **first aim** or intent is **social good**.

- ✓ High-vibe service providers know the time is right. They have the skills, experience, and drive to make it happen.

Overall, high-vibe service providers take inspired action to create phenomenal results for their clients, joint venture partners, support team, and for themselves. It's no wonder they're successful and able to amplify their impact and influence, it all lines up for them (see Way 8)—their mission, purpose, and service!

About the Author

You could say MaryAnn D'Ambrosio, MBA, Ph.D., is energetically charged. She swapped a lifelong corporate career in the power industry for one where she sparks entrepreneurs, business leaders, and service professionals to leap without limits and land in a place where they will grow and prosper.

How does she do it?

As a gifted energy healer, speaker, and coach, she understands the fields of energy that connect us all, and she takes audiences through a process that instantly unites their personal strengths with their passion for success. An inspirational, engaging speaker, MaryAnn leads seminars that are at once thoughtful and thought provoking. The audience naturally awakens to a deeper understanding and a new way of approaching business and life that brings about elegant breakthroughs. Transmuting AHA moments into awareness is profound, and under MaryAnn's guidance the nudges are soft, and the results powerful and transformative!

To learn more about MaryAnn, visit

 LeapWithoutLimits.com

Y.E.S. You Can . . .

Dramatically Increase Your Platform Performance & Prosperity!

Get more clients to Y.E.S.! *Your Energetic Signal* shows you how!

As The Event Prosperity Coach, MaryAnn D'Ambrosio helps speakers get the most out of their presentations energetically by aligning their *Y.E.S. (Your Energetic Signal)*.

Aligned speakers and presenters see phenomenal results compared to what they've done in the past! Here's why . . . being energetically aligned on all levels, supercharges you to fully embody your purpose, gifts, and talents while successfully communicating - transmitting your magnetic message that draws in ideal clients.

It's Time to Energize Your Results . . .
Accelerate Your Success!

Align Your Energetic Signal **so potential clients consistently say, "Yes!"**

 LeapWithoutLimits.com/Align

Begin Today . . .

Discover a More Vibrant Creative YOU!!

You know you need to relax and breathe – yet, you're trapped in busyness. Instead of feeling overwhelmed and running from one thing to another, wouldn't it be great to be clear, focused and have more time for yourself and the relationships that really matter in your life?

e-Flashcards for the Soul™

There's a way to quickly set the tone for the day by accessing daily inspiration and guidance through Flashcards For The Soul™ e-cards. The e-cards are your secret partner for creative energy and vibrant aliveness.

To learn more visit:

 eFlashcardsForTheSoul.com

Collect them all!

Look for more *21 Ways*™ books at
21WaysBooks.com

www.ingramcontent.com/pod-product-compliance
Lightning Source LLC
Chambersburg PA
CBHW052103070526
44584CB0001７B/2308